Mindfulness

HBR EMOTIONAL INTELLIGENCE SERIES

HBR Emotional Intelligence Series

How to be human at work

The HBR Emotional Intelligence Series features smart, essential reading on the human side of professional life from the pages of *Harvard Business Review*.

Empathy

Happiness

Mindfulness

Resilience

Other books on emotional intelligence from *Harvard Business Review*:

HBR's 10 Must Reads on Emotional Intelligence

HBR Guide to Emotional Intelligence

Mindfulness

HBR EMOTIONAL INTELLIGENCE SERIES

Harvard Business Review Press

Boston, Massachusetts

Copyright 2017
Harvard Business School Publishing Corporation
All rights reserved
Printed in the United States of America

10 9 8 7 6 5

The web addresses referenced in this book were live and correct at the time of the book's publication but may be subject to change.

Library of Congress Cataloging-in-Publication Data

Title: Mindfulness.
Other titles: HBR emotional intelligence series.
Description: Boston, Massachusetts : Harvard Business Review Press, [2017] | Series: HBR emotional intelligence series
Identifiers: LCCN 2016056277 | ISBN 9781633693197 (pbk. : alk. paper)
Subjects: LCSH: Mindfulness (Psychology) | Mindfulness-based cognitive therapy.
Classification: LCC BF637.M56 M56 2017 | DDC 152.4—dc23 LC record available at https://lccn.loc.gov/2016056277

ISBN: 978-1-63369-319-7
eISBN: 978-1-63369-320-3

The paper used in this publication meets the requirements of the American National Standard for Permanence of Paper for Publications and Documents in Libraries and Archives Z39.48-1992.

Contents

Contents

Mindfulness

HBR EMOTIONAL INTELLIGENCE SERIES

1

Mindfulness in the Age of Complexity

An interview with Ellen Langer by Alison Beard

Over nearly four decades, Ellen Langer's research on mindfulness has greatly influenced thinking across a range of fields, from behavioral economics to positive psychology. It reveals that by paying attention to what's going on around us, instead of operating on autopilot, we can reduce stress, unlock creativity, and boost performance. Her "counterclockwise" experiments, for example, demonstrated that elderly men could improve their health by simply acting as if it were 20 years earlier. In this interview with senior editor Alison Beard, Langer applies her thinking to leadership and management in an age of increasing chaos.

HBR: *Let's start with the basics. What, exactly, is mindfulness? How do you define it?*

Langer: Mindfulness is the process of actively noticing new things. When you do that, it puts you in the present. It makes you more sensitive to context and perspective. It's the essence of engagement. And it's energy-begetting, not energy-consuming. The mistake most people make is to assume it's stressful and exhausting—all this thinking. But what's stressful is all the mindless negative evaluations we make and the worry that we'll find problems and not be able to solve them.

We all seek stability. We want to hold things still, thinking that if we do, we can control them. But since everything is always changing, that doesn't work. Actually, it causes you to lose control.

Take work processes. When people say, "This is the way to do it," that's not true. There are always many ways, and the way you choose should depend on the current context. You can't solve to-day's problems with yesterday's solutions. So when someone says, "Learn this so it's second nature," let a bell go off in your head, because that means mindlessness. The rules you were given were the rules that worked for the person who created them, and the more different you are from that person, the worse they're going to work for you. When you're mindful, rules, routines, and goals guide you; they don't govern you.

What are some of the specific benefits of being more mindful, according to your research?

Better performance, for one. We did a study with symphony musicians, who, it turns out, are bored to death. They're playing the same pieces over and over again, and yet it's a high-status job that they can't easily walk away from. So we had groups of them perform. Some were told to replicate a previous performance they'd liked—that is, to play pretty mindlessly. Others were told to make their individual performance new in subtle ways—to play mindfully. Remember: This wasn't jazz, so the changes were very subtle indeed. But when we played recordings of the symphonies for people who knew nothing about the study, they overwhelmingly preferred the mindfully played pieces. So here we had a group performance where everybody was doing their own thing, and it was better. There's this view that if you let everyone do their own thing, chaos will reign. When people are doing their own thing in a rebellious way, yes, it might. But if everyone is working in the same context and is fully present, there's no reason why you shouldn't get a superior coordinated performance.

There are many other advantages to mindfulness. It's easier to pay attention. You remember more of what you've done. You're more creative. You're able to take advantage of opportunities when they present themselves. You avert the danger not yet arisen. You like people better, and people like you better, because you're less evaluative. You're more charismatic.

The idea of procrastination and regret can go away, because if you know why you're doing something, you don't take yourself to task for not doing something else. If you're fully present when you decide to prioritize this task or work at this firm or create this product or pursue this strategy, why would you regret it?

I've been studying this for nearly 40 years, and for almost any measure, we find that mindfulness generates a more positive result. That makes sense when you realize it's a superordinate variable. No matter what you're doing—eating a sandwich, doing an interview, working on some gizmo, writing a report—you're doing it mindfully or mindlessly. When it's the former, it leaves an imprint on what you do. At the very highest levels of any field—

Fortune 50 CEOs, the most impressive artists and musicians, the top athletes, the best teachers and mechanics—you'll find mindful people, because that's the only way to get there.

How have you shown a link between mindfulness and innovation?

With Gabriel Hammond, a graduate student, I ran a study where we asked participants to come up with new uses for products that had failed. We primed one group for mindlessness by telling them how the product had fallen short of its original intended use—to cite a famous example from 3M, a failed glue. We primed the other for mindfulness by simply describing the product's properties— a substance that adheres for only a short amount of time. Of course, the most creative ideas for new uses came from the second group.

I'm an artist as well as a researcher, writer, and consultant—each activity informs the others for me—and I got the idea to study mindfulness and mistakes when I was painting. I looked up and saw I was using ocher when I'd meant to use magenta, so I started trying to fix it. But then I realized I'd made the decision to use magenta only seconds before. People do this all the time. You start with uncertainty, you make a decision, and if you make a mistake, it's a calamity. But the path you were following was just a decision. You can change it at any time, and maybe an alternative will turn out better. When you're mindful, mistakes become friends.

How does being mindful make someone more charismatic?

We've shown this in a few studies. An early one was with magazine salespeople: The mindful ones sold more and were rated as more likable by buyers. More recently, we've looked at the bind that women executives face: If they act in strong, stereotypically masculine ways, they're seen as bitchy, but if they act feminine, they're seen as weak and not leadership material. So we asked two groups of women to give persuasive speeches. One group was told to act masculine, the other to act feminine. Then half of each group was instructed to give their speech mindfully, and we found that audiences preferred the mindful speakers, regardless of what gender role they were playing out.

And mindfulness also makes you less judgmental about others?

Yes. We all have a tendency to mindlessly pigeonhole people: He's rigid. She's impulsive. But when you freeze someone in that way, you don't get the chance to enjoy a relationship with them or use their talents. Mindfulness helps you to appreciate why people behave the way they do. It makes sense to them at the time, or else they wouldn't do it.

We did a study in which we asked people to rate their own character traits—the things they would most like to change and the things they most valued about themselves—and we found a big irony. The traits that people valued tended to be positive versions of the ones they wanted to change. So the reason I personally can't stop being impulsive is that I value being spontaneous. That means if you want to change my behavior, you'll have to persuade me not to like spontaneity. But chances are that when you see me from this proper perspective— spontaneous rather than impulsive—you won't want to change me.

Mindful management

What else can managers do to be more mindful?

One tactic is to imagine that your thoughts are totally transparent. If they were, you wouldn't think awful things about other people. You'd find a way to understand their perspective.

And when you're upset about something—maybe someone turned in an assignment late or didn't do it the way you wanted—ask yourself, "Is it a tragedy or an inconvenience?" It's probably the latter. Most of the things that get us upset are.

I also tell people to think about work/life *integration*, not balance. "Balance" suggests that the two are opposite and have nothing in common. But that's not true. They're both mostly about people. There are stresses in both. There are schedules to be met. If you keep them separate, you don't learn to transfer what you do successfully in one domain to the other. When we're mindful, we realize that categories are person constructed and don't limit us.

Remember, too, that stress is not a function of events; it's a function of the view you take of events. You think a particular thing is going to happen and that when it does, it's going to be awful. But prediction is an illusion. We can't know what's going to happen. So give yourself five reasons you won't lose the job. Then think of five reasons why, if you did, it would be an advantage—new opportunities, more time with family, et cetera. Now you've gone from thinking it's definitely going to happen to thinking maybe it will and even if it does, you'll be OK.

If you feel overwhelmed by your responsibilities, use the same approach. Question the belief that you're the only one who can do it, that there's only one way to do it, and that the company will collapse if you don't do it. When you open your views to be mindful, the stress just dissipates.

Mindfulness helps you realize that there are no positive or negative outcomes. There's A, B, C, D, and more, each with its challenges and opportunities.

Give me some scenarios, and I'll explain how mindfulness helps.

I'm the leader of a team in dissent. People are arguing vehemently for different strategies, and I have to decide on one.

There's an old story about two people coming before a judge. One guy tells his side of the story, and the judge says, "That's right." The other guy tells his side of the story, and the judge says, "That's right." They say, "We can't both be right." And the judge says, "That's right." We have this mindless notion to settle disputes with a choice between this way or that way, or a compromise. But win-win solutions can almost always be sought. Instead of letting people lock into their positions, go back and open it up. Have opponents play the debate from the other side so that they realize there are good arguments either way. Then find a way for both of them to be right.

I'm an executive with lots of commitments who's facing a personal crisis.

If I couldn't do this interview because I was having a problem at home, I would say, "Alison, I hope you'll forgive me, but my mind is elsewhere right now because I'm having this crisis." And you might say, "Oh, no, I had a crisis last week. It's OK. I understand." And then, when the crisis was over, we could come back to what we were doing, but with a whole new relationship, which would set us up for all sorts of good things in the future.

I'm a boss giving a review to an underperforming employee.

Make clear that the evaluation is *your* perspective, not a universal one, which opens up the dialogue. Let's say a student or a worker adds one and one and gets one. The teacher or employer can just say "Wrong," or he can try to figure out how the person got to one. Then the worker says, "If you add one wad of chewing gum to another wad, one plus one equals one." Now the boss has learned something.

As a leader, you can walk around as if you're God and get everybody to quiver. But then you're not going to learn anything, because they're not going to tell you, and you're going to be lonely and unhappy. It doesn't have to be lonely at the top. You can be there and be open.

How do you create a more mindful organization?

When I'm doing consulting work with companies, I usually start by showing everyone how mindless they are and what they're missing as a result. You can be mindless only if two conditions are met: You've found the very best way of doing things, and nothing changes. Of course, those conditions can't be met. So if you're going to work, you should be there and notice things. Then I explain that there are alternative ways of getting anywhere, and in fact, you can't even be sure that the destination you've chosen is ultimately where you'll want to be. Everything looks different from different perspectives.

I tell leaders they should make not knowing OK—I don't know, you don't know, nobody knows—rather than acting like they know, so everyone else pretends *they* know, which leads to all sorts of discomfort and anxiety. Eliminate zero-accident policies. If you have a zero-accident policy, you're going to have a maximum-lying policy. Get people to ask, "Why? What are the benefits of doing it this way versus another way?" When you do that, everyone relaxes a little, and you're all better able to see and take advantage of opportunities.

I was working with a nursing home years ago, and a nurse walked in, complaining that one of the residents didn't want to go to the dining room. She wanted to stay in her room and eat peanut butter. So I butted in and said, "What's wrong with that?" Her answer was "What if everybody wants to do it?" And I said, "Well, if everybody did it, you'd save a lot of money on food. But, more seriously, it would tell you something about how the food is being prepared or served. If it's only one person occasionally, what's the big deal? If it happens all the time, there's an opportunity here."

I imagine you don't like checklists?

The first time you go through a checklist, it's fine. But after that, most people tend to do it mindlessly. So in aviation you have flaps up, throttle open, anti-ice off. But if snow is coming and the anti-ice is off, the plane crashes.

Checklists aren't bad if they require qualitative information to be obtained in that moment. For example, "Please note the weather conditions. Based on these conditions, should the anti-ice be on or off?" or "How is the patient's skin color different from yesterday?" If you ask questions that encourage mindfulness, you bring people into the present and you're more likely to avoid an accident.

Mindful, qualitative comments help in interpersonal relationships, too, by the way. If you're giving a compliment, "You look great" is not nearly as effective as something like "Your eyes are sparkling today." To say that, you have to be there, and people will recognize and appreciate it.

Mindfulness and focus

The business environment has changed a lot since you began studying mindfulness. It's more complex and uncertain. We have new data and analysis coming at us all the time. So mindfulness becomes more important for navigating the chaos—but the chaos makes it a lot harder to be mindful.

I think chaos is a perception. People say that there's too much information, and I would say that there's no more information now than there was before. The difference is that people believe they have to know it—that the more information they have, the better the product is going to be and the more money the company is going to make. I don't think it depends as much on the amount of information someone has as on the way it's taken in. And that needs to be mindfully.

How has technology changed our ability to be mindful? Is it a help or a hindrance?

Again, one can bring mindfulness to anything. We've studied multitasking and found that if you're open and keep the boundaries loose, it can be an advantage. The information from one thing can help you with another. I think what we should do is learn from the way technology is fun and compelling and build that into our work.

HBR recently published an article on the importance of focus in which the author, Daniel Goleman, talks about the need for both exploration and exploitation. How do you balance mindfulness—constantly looking for the new—with the ability to buckle down and get things done?

Vigilance, or very focused attention, is probably mindless. If I'm racing through the woods on horseback, watching the branches so that I don't get hit in the face, I might miss the boulder on the ground, so then my horse stumbles and I'm thrown off. But I don't think that's what Dan means by focus. What you want is a soft openness—to be attentive to the things you're doing but not single-minded, because then you're missing other opportunities.

We hear the management community talking more about mindfulness now. When did you realize that the ideas you've been studying for decades had become mainstream?

I was at a party, and two different people came up to me and said, "Your mindfulness is everywhere."

Of course, I just saw a new film that starts with someone going around Harvard Square asking people what mindfulness is, and nobody knows. So there's still a lot of work to do.

What are you working on next?

The Langer Mindfulness Institute works in three arenas: health, aging, and the workplace. In health we want to see just how far we can push the mind-body notion. Years ago we did studies on chambermaids (who lost weight after being told their work was exercise) and vision (where people did better on eye tests that had them work up from large letters at the bottom to small ones at the top, creating the expectation that they would be able to read them). Now we're trying a mindfulness cure on many diseases that people think are uncontrollable to see if we can at least ameliorate the symptoms. We're also doing counterclockwise retreats around the world, starting in San Miguel de Allende, Mexico, using research-proven techniques to help people live boldly. And we're doing conferences and consulting on work/life integration, mindful leadership and strategy processes, stress reduction, and innovation, with companies such as Thorlo and Santander and NGOs such as CARE and Vermont's Energy Action Network.

I'm told that I drive my students crazy because I'm always coming up with new ideas. I'm thinking about maybe a mindfulness camp for children. One exercise might be to take a group of 20 kids and keep dividing them into subsets—male/female, younger/older, dark hair/light hair, wearing black/not wearing black—until they realize that everyone is unique. As I've said for 30 years, the best way to decrease prejudice is to increase discrimination. We would also play games and midway through mix up the teams. Or maybe we'd give each child a chance to rewrite the rules of the game, so it becomes clear that performance is only a reflection of one's ability under certain circumstances.

You know, if they allowed three serves in tennis, I would be a much better player.

What's the one thing about mindfulness you'd like every executive to remember?

It's going to sound corny, but I believe it fully: Life consists only of moments, nothing more than that. So if you make the moment matter, it all matters. You can be mindful, you can be mindless. You can win, you can lose. The worst case is to be mindless and lose. So when you're doing anything, be mindful, notice new things, make it meaningful to you, and you'll prosper.

ELLEN LANGER, PHD, is a professor of psychology at Harvard University and founder of the Langer Mindfulness Institute. ALISON BEARD is a senior editor at *Harvard Business Review*.

Reprinted from *Harvard Business Review*, March 2014 (product #R1403D).

2

Mindfulness Can Literally Change Your Brain

By Christina Congleton, Britta K. Hölzel, and Sara W. Lazar

The business world is abuzz with mindfulness. But perhaps you haven't heard that the hype is backed by hard science. Recent research provides strong evidence that practicing nonjudgmental, present-moment awareness (aka mindfulness) changes the brain, and it does so in ways that anyone working in today's complex business environment— and certainly every leader—should know about.[1]

We contributed to this research in 2011 with a study on participants who completed an eight-week mindfulness program.[2] We observed significant increases in the density of their gray matter. In the years since, neuroscience laboratories from around the world have also investigated ways in which meditation, one key way to practice mindfulness, changes the brain. This year, a team of scientists from the University of British Columbia and the Chemnitz University of Technology were able to pool data from more than 20 studies to determine which areas of the brain are consistently affected.[3] They identified at least eight different regions. Here we will focus on two that we believe to be of particular interest to business professionals.

The first is the anterior cingulate cortex (ACC), a structure located deep inside the forehead, behind the brain's frontal lobe. The ACC is associated with self-regulation, meaning the ability to purposefully direct attention and behavior, suppress inappropriate knee-jerk responses, and switch strategies flexibly.[4] People with damage to the ACC show impulsivity and unchecked aggression, and those with impaired connections between this and other brain regions perform poorly on tests of mental flexibility:

They hold onto ineffective problem-solving strategies rather than adapting their behavior.[5] Meditators, on the other hand, demonstrate superior performance on tests of self-regulation, resisting distractions and making correct answers more often than non-meditators.[6] They also show more activity in the ACC than nonmeditators.[7] In addition to self-regulation, the ACC is associated with learning from past experience to support optimal decision making.[8] Scientists point out that the ACC may be particularly important in the face of uncertain and fast-changing conditions.

The second brain region we want to highlight is the hippocampus, a region that showed increased amounts of gray matter in the brains of our 2011 mindfulness program participants. This seahorse-shaped area is buried inside the temple on each side of the brain and is part of the limbic system, a set of inner structures associated with emotion and memory. It is covered in receptors for the stress hormone cortisol, and studies have shown that it can be damaged by chronic stress, contributing to a harmful spiral in the body.[9] Indeed, people with stress-related disorders like depression and PTSD tend to have a smaller hippocampus.[10] All of this points to the importance of this brain area in resilience—another key skill in the current high-demand business world.

These findings are just the beginning of the story. Neuroscientists have also shown that practicing mindfulness affects brain areas related to perception, body awareness, pain tolerance, emotion regulation, introspection, complex thinking, and sense of self. While more research is needed to document these changes over time and to understand underlying mechanisms, the converging evidence is compelling.

Mindfulness should no longer be considered a "nice to have" for executives. It's a "must have": a way to keep our brains healthy, to support self-regulation and effective decision-making capabilities, and to protect ourselves from toxic stress. It can be integrated into one's religious or spiritual life or practiced as a form of secular mental training. When we take a seat, take a breath, and commit to being mindful— particularly when we gather with others who are doing the same—we have the potential to be changed.

CHRISTINA CONGLETON is a leadership and change consultant at Axon Leadership and has researched stress and the brain at Massachusetts General Hospital and the University of Denver. She holds a master's in human development and psychology from Harvard University. BRITTA K. HÖLZEL conducts MRI research to investigate the neural mechanisms of mindfulness practice. Previously a research fellow at Massachusetts General Hospital and Harvard Medical School, she currently works at the Technical University Munich. She holds a doctorate in psychology from Giessen University in Germany. SARA W. LAZAR is an associate researcher in the psychiatry department at Massachusetts General Hospital and an assistant professor in psychology at Harvard Medical School. The focus of her research is to elucidate the neural mechanisms underlying the beneficial effects of yoga and meditation, both in clinical settings and in healthy individuals.

Notes

1. S. N. Banhoo, "How Meditation May Change the Brain," *New York Times*, January 28, 2011.

2. B. K. Hölzel et al., "Mindfulness Practice Leads to Increases in Regional Brain Gray Matter Density," *Psychiatry Research* 191, no. 1 (January 30, 2011): 36–43.

3. K. C. Fox et al., "Is Meditation Associated with Altered Brain Structure? A Systematic Review and Meta-Analysis of Morphometric Neuroimaging in Meditation Practitioners," *Neuroscience and Biobehavioral Reviews* 43 (June 2014): 48–73.

4. M. Posner et al., "The Anterior Cingulate Gyrus and the Mechanism of Self-Regulation," *Cognitive, Affective, & Behavioral Neuroscience* 7, no. 4 (December 2007): 391–395.

5. O. Devinsky et al., "Contributions of Anterior Cingulate Cortex to Behavior," *Brain* 118, part 1 (February 1995): 279–306; and A. M. Hogan et al., "Impact of Frontal White Matter Lesions on Performance Monitoring: ERP Evidence for Cortical Disconnection," *Brain* 129, part 8 (August 2006): 2177–2188.

6. P. A. van den Hurk et al., "Greater Efficiency in Attentional Processing Related to Mindfulness Meditation," *Quarterly Journal of Experimental Psychology* 63, no. 6 (June 2010): 1168–1180.

7. B. K. Hölzel et al., "Differential Engagement of Anterior Cingulate and Adjacent Medial Frontal Cortex in Adept Meditators and Non-meditators," *Neuroscience Letters* 421, no. 1 (June 21): 16–21.

8. S. W. Kennerley et al., "Optimal Decision Making and the Anterior Cingulate Cortex," *Nature Neuroscience* 9 (June 18, 2006): 940–947.

9. B. S. McEwen and P. J. Gianaros. "Stress- and Allostasis-Induced Brain Plasticity," *Annual Review of Medicine* 62 (February 2011): 431–445.
10. Y. I. Sheline, "Neuroimaging Studies of Mood Disorder Effects on the Brain." *Biological Psychiatry* 54, no. 3 (August 1, 2003): 338–352; and T. V. Gurvits et al., "Magnetic Resonance Imaging Study of Hippocampal Volume in Chronic, Combat-Related Posttraumatic Stress Disorder," *Biological Psychiatry* 40, no. 11 (December 1, 1996): 1091–1099.

Adapted from content posted on hbr.org on
January 8, 2015 (#H01T5A).

3

How to Practice Mindfulness Throughout Your Work Day

By Rasmus Hougaard and Jacqueline Carter

You probably know the feeling all too well: You arrive at the office with a clear plan for the day, and then, in what feels like just a moment, you find yourself on your way back home. Nine or ten hours have passed but you've accomplished only a few of your priorities. And, most likely, you can't even remember exactly what you did all day. If this sounds familiar, don't worry: You're not alone. Research shows that people spend nearly 47% of their waking hours thinking about something other than what they're doing.[1] In other words, many of us operate on autopilot.

Add to this that we have entered what many people are calling the "attention economy." In the attention economy, the ability to maintain focus and concentration is every bit as important as technical or management skills. And because leaders must be able to absorb and synthesize a growing flood of information in order to make good decisions, they're hit particularly hard by this emerging trend.

The good news is you can train your brain to focus better by incorporating mindfulness exercises throughout your day. Based on our experience with thousands of leaders in more than 250 organizations, here are some guidelines for becoming a more focused and mindful leader.

First, start off your day right. Researchers have found that we release the most stress hormones within minutes after waking.[2] Why? Because thinking of the day ahead triggers our fight-or-flight instinct and releases cortisol into our blood. Instead, try this: When you wake up, spend two minutes in your bed simply noticing your breath. As thoughts about the day pop into your mind, let them go and return to your breath.

Next, when you get to the office, take 10 minutes at your desk or in your car to boost your brain with the following short mindfulness practice before you dive into activity. Close your eyes, relax, and sit upright. Place your full focus on your breath. Simply maintain an ongoing flow of attention on the experience of your breathing: Inhale, exhale; inhale, exhale. To help your focus stay on your breathing, count silently at each exhalation. Any time you find your mind distracted, simply release the distraction by returning your focus to your breath. Most important, allow yourself to enjoy these minutes. Throughout the rest of the day, other people and competing urgencies will fight for your attention. But for these 10 minutes, your attention is all your own.

Once you finish this practice and get ready to start working, mindfulness can help increase your effectiveness. Two skills define a mindful mind: *focus* and *awareness*. Focus is the ability to concentrate on what you're doing in the moment, while awareness is the ability to recognize and release unnecessary distractions as they arise. Understand that mindfulness is not just a sedentary practice; it is about developing a sharp, clear mind. And mindfulness in action is a great alternative to the illusory practice of multitasking. Mindful working means applying focus and awareness to everything you do from the moment you enter the office. Focus on the task at hand, and recognize and release internal and external distractions as they arise. In this way, mindfulness helps increase effectiveness, decrease mistakes, and even enhance creativity.

To better understand the power of focus and awareness, consider an affliction that touches nearly all of us: email addiction. Emails have a way of seducing our attention and redirecting it to lower-priority tasks because completing small, quickly accomplished tasks releases dopamine, a pleasurable hormone, in our brains. This release makes us addicted to email and compromises our concentration. Instead, apply mindfulness when opening your inbox. *Focus* on what is important and maintain *awareness* of what is merely noise. To get a better start to your day, avoid checking your email first thing in the morning. Doing so will help you sidestep an onslaught of distractions and short-term problems during a time of day that holds the potential for exceptional focus and creativity.

As the day moves on and the inevitable back-to-back meetings start, mindfulness can help you lead shorter, more effective meetings. To avoid entering a meeting with a wandering mind, take two minutes to practice mindfulness, which you can do en route. Even better, let the first two minutes of the meeting be silent, allowing everybody to arrive both physically and mentally. Then, if possible, end the meeting five minutes before the hour to allow all participants a mindful transition to their next appointment.

As the day progresses and your brain starts to tire, mindfulness can help you stay sharp and avoid poor decisions. After lunch, set a timer on your phone to ring every hour. When the timer rings, cease your current activity and do one minute of mindfulness practice. These mindful performance breaks will help keep you from resorting to autopilot and lapsing into action addiction.

Finally, as the day comes to an end and you start your commute home, apply mindfulness. For at least 10 minutes of the commute, turn off your phone, shut off the radio, and simply be. Let go of any thoughts that arise. Attend to your breath. Doing so will allow you to let go of the stresses of the day so you can return home and be fully present with your family.

Mindfulness is not about living life in slow motion. It's about enhancing focus and awareness both in work and in life. It's about stripping away distractions and staying on track with both individual and organizational, goals. Take control of your own mindfulness: Test these tips for 14 days, and see what they do for you.

RASMUS HOUGAARD is the founder and managing director of The Potential Project, a leading global provider of corporate-based mindfulness solutions. He is a coauthor with Jacqueline Carter of *One Second Ahead: Enhance Your Performance at Work with Mindfulness*. JACQUELINE CARTER is a partner with The Potential Project and has worked with leaders around the globe, including executives from Sony, American Express, RBC, and KPMG.

Notes

1. S. Bradt, "Wandering Mind Not a Happy Mind," *Harvard Gazette*, November 11, 2010.
2. J. C. Pruessner et al., "Free Cortisol Levels After Awakening: A Reliable Biological Marker for the Assessment of Adrenocortical Activity," *Life Sciences* 61, no. 26 (November 1997): 2539–2549.

Adapted from content posted on hbr.org on
March 4, 2016 (#H02OTU).

4

Resilience for
the Rest of Us

By Daniel Goleman

There are two ways to become more resilient: one by talking to yourself, the other by retraining your brain.

If you've suffered a major failure, take the sage advice given by psychologist Martin Seligman in the HBR article "Building Resilience" (April 2011). Talk to yourself. Give yourself a cognitive intervention, and counter defeatist thinking with an optimistic attitude. Challenge your downbeat thinking, and replace it with a positive outlook.

Fortunately, major failures come along rarely in life.

But what about bouncing back from the more frequent annoying screwups, minor setbacks, and irritating upsets that are routine in any leader's life? Resilience is, again, the answer—but with a different flavor. You need to retrain your brain.

The brain has a very different mechanism for bouncing back from the cumulative toll of daily hassles. And with a little effort, you can upgrade its ability to snap back from life's downers.

Whenever we get so upset that we say or do something we later regret (and who doesn't now and then?), that's a sure sign that our amygdala—the brain's radar for danger and the trigger for the fight-or-flight response—has hijacked the brain's executive centers in the prefrontal cortex. The neural key to resilience lies in how quickly we recover from that hijacked state.

The circuitry that brings us back to full energy and focus after an amygdala hijack concentrates in the left side of our prefrontal area, says Richard Davidson, a neuroscientist at the University of Wisconsin. He's also found that when we're distressed, there's heightened activity on the right side of the prefrontal area. Each of us has a characteristic level of left/right activity that predicts our daily mood range—if we're tilted to the right, more upsets; if to the left, we're quicker to recover from distress of all kinds.

To tackle this in the workplace, Davidson teamed with the CEO of a high-pressure, 24/7, biotech startup and meditation expert Jon Kabat-Zinn of the University of Massachusetts Medical School. Kabat-Zinn offered the employees at the biotech outfit instruction in mindfulness, an attention-training method that teaches the brain to register anything happening in the present moment with full focus—but without reacting.

The instructions are simple:

1. Find a quiet, private place where you can be undistracted for a few minutes. For instance, close your office door and mute your phone.

2. Sit comfortably, with your back straight but relaxed.

3. Focus your awareness on your breath, staying attentive to the sensations of the inhalation and exhalation, and start again on the next breath.

4. Do not judge your breathing or try to change it in any way.

5. See anything else that comes to mind as a distraction—thoughts, sounds, whatever. Let them go and return your attention to your breath.

After eight weeks and an average of 30 minutes a day practicing mindfulness, the employees had shifted their ratio from tilted toward the stressed-out right side to leaning toward the resilient left side. What's more, they said they remembered what they loved about their work: They got in touch with what had brought them energy in the first place.

To get the full benefit of mindfulness, a daily practice of 20 to 30 minutes works best. Think of it like a mental exercise routine. It can be very helpful to have guided instructions, but the key is to find a slot for the practice in your daily routine. (There are even instructions for using a long drive as your practice session.)

Mindfulness has steadily been gaining credence among hard-nosed executives. There are centers where mindfulness instruction has been tailored to businesspeople, from tony resorts like Miraval Resort in Arizona to programs in mindful leadership at the University of Massachusetts Medical School. Google University has been offering a course in mindfulness to employees for years.

Might you benefit from tuning up your brain's resilience circuitry by learning to practice mindfulness? Among high-performing executives, the effects of stress can be subtle. My colleagues Richard Boyatzis and Annie McKee suggest as a rough diagnostic of leadership stress asking yourself, "Do I have a vague sense of unease, restlessness, or the feeling that life

is not great (a higher standard than 'good enough')?"
A bit of mindfulness might put your mind at ease.

DANIEL GOLEMAN is a codirector of the Consortium for
Research on Emotional Intelligence in Organizations at Rut-
gers University, coauthor of *Primal Leadership: Leading
with Emotional Intelligence* (Harvard Business Review Press,
2013), and author of *The Brain and Emotional Intelligence:
New Insights*.

Adapted from content posted on hbr.org on
March 4, 2016.

5

Emotional Agility

*How Effective Leaders Manage
Their Thoughts and Feelings*

By Susan David and Christina Congleton

Sixteen thousand—that's how many words we speak, on average, each day. So imagine how many unspoken ones course through our minds. Most of them are not facts but evaluations and judgments entwined with emotions—some positive and helpful (*I've worked hard and I can ace this presentation; This issue is worth speaking up about; The new VP seems approachable*), others negative and less so (*He's purposely ignoring me; I'm going to make a fool of myself; I'm a fake*).

The prevailing wisdom says that difficult thoughts and feelings have no place at the office: Executives, and particularly leaders, should be either stoic or cheerful; they must project confidence and damp down any negativity bubbling up inside them. But that goes against basic biology. All healthy human beings have an inner stream of thoughts and feelings that include criticism, doubt, and fear. That's just our minds doing the job they were designed to do: trying to anticipate and solve problems and avoid potential pitfalls.

In our people-strategy consulting practice advising companies around the world, we see leaders stumble not because they *have* undesirable thoughts and feelings—that's inevitable—but because they get *hooked* by them, like fish caught on a line. This happens in one of two ways. They buy into the thoughts, treating them like facts (*It was the same in my last job . . . I've been a failure my whole career*), and avoid situations that evoke them (*I'm not going to take on that new challenge*). Or, usually at the behest of their supporters, they challenge the existence of the thoughts and try to rationalize them away (*I shouldn't have thoughts like this . . . I know I'm not a total failure*), and perhaps force themselves into similar situations, even when those go against their core values and goals (*Take on that new assignment—you've got to get over this*). In either case, they are paying too much attention to their internal chatter and allowing it to sap important cognitive resources that could be put to better use.

This is a common problem, often perpetuated by popular self-management strategies. We regularly see executives with recurring emotional challenges at work—anxiety about priorities, jealousy of others' success, fear of rejection, distress over perceived slights—who have devised techniques to "fix" them: positive affirmations, prioritized to-do lists, immersion in certain tasks. But when we ask how long the challenges have persisted, the answer might be 10 years, 20 years, or since childhood.

Clearly, those techniques don't work—in fact, ample research shows that attempting to minimize or ignore thoughts and emotions serves only to amplify them. In a famous study led by the late Daniel Wegner, a Harvard professor, participants who were told to avoid thinking about white bears had trouble doing so; later, when the ban was lifted, they thought about white bears much more than the control group did. Anyone who has dreamed of chocolate cake and french fries while following a strict diet understands this phenomenon.

Effective leaders don't buy into *or* try to suppress their inner experiences. Instead they approach them in a mindful, values-driven, and productive way—developing what we call *emotional agility*. In our complex, fast-changing knowledge economy, this ability to manage one's thoughts and feelings is essential to business success. Numerous studies, from the University of London professor Frank Bond and others, show that emotional agility can help people alleviate stress, reduce errors, become more innovative, and improve job performance.

We've worked with leaders in various industries to build this critical skill, and here we offer four practices—adapted from Acceptance and Commitment Therapy (ACT), originally developed by the University of Nevada psychologist Steven C. Hayes—that are designed to help you do the same: Recognize your patterns; label your thoughts and emotions; accept them; and act on your values.

Fish on a line

Let's start with two case studies. Cynthia is a senior corporate lawyer with two young children. She used to feel intense guilt about missed opportunities—both at the office, where her peers worked 80 hours a week while she worked 50, and at home, where she was often too distracted or tired to fully engage with her husband and children. One nagging voice in her head told her she'd have to be a better employee or risk career failure; another told her to be a better mother or risk neglecting her family. Cynthia wished that at least one of the voices would shut up. But neither would, and in response she failed to put up her hand for exciting new prospects at the office and compulsively checked messages on her phone during family dinners.

Jeffrey, a rising-star executive at a leading consumer goods company, had a different problem. Intelligent, talented, and ambitious, he was often angry—at bosses who disregarded his views, subordinates who didn't follow orders, or colleagues who didn't pull their weight. He had lost his temper several times at work and been warned to get it under control. But when he tried, he felt that he was shutting off a core part of his personality, and he became even angrier and more upset.

These smart, successful leaders were hooked by their negative thoughts and emotions. Cynthia was absorbed by guilt; Jeffrey was exploding with anger.

Cynthia told the voices to go away; Jeffrey bottled his frustration. Both were trying to avoid the discomfort they felt. They were being controlled by their inner experience, attempting to control it, or switching between the two.

Getting unhooked

Fortunately, both Cynthia and Jeffrey realized that they couldn't go on—at least not successfully and happily—without more-effective inner strategies. We coached them to adopt the four practices:

Recognize your patterns

The first step in developing emotional agility is to notice when you've been hooked by your thoughts and feelings. That's hard to do, but there are certain telltale signs. One is that your thinking becomes rigid and repetitive. For example, Cynthia began to see that her self-recriminations played like a broken record, repeating the same messages over and over again. Another is that the story your mind is telling seems old, like a rerun of some past experience. Jeffrey noticed that his attitude toward certain colleagues (*He's incompetent; There's no way I'm letting anyone speak to me like that*) was quite familiar. In fact, he had experienced something similar in his previous job—and in the one before that. The source of trouble was not just Jeffrey's environment but his own patterns of thought and feeling. You have to realize that you're stuck before you can initiate change.

Label your thoughts and emotions

When you're hooked, the attention you give your thoughts and feelings crowds your mind; there's no room to examine them. One strategy that may help you consider your situation more objectively is the simple act of labeling. Just as you call a spade a spade, call a thought a thought and an emotion an emotion. *I'm not doing enough at work or at home* becomes *I'm having the thought that I'm not doing enough at work or at home.* Similarly, *My coworker is wrong—he makes me so angry* becomes *I'm having the thought that my coworker is wrong, and I'm feeling anger.* Labeling allows you to see your thoughts and feelings for what they are: transient sources of data that may or may not prove helpful. Humans are psychologically able to take this helicopter view of private experiences, and mounting scientific evidence shows that simple, straightforward mindfulness practice like this not only improves behavior and well-being but also promotes beneficial biological changes in the brain and at the cellular level. As Cynthia started to slow down and label her thoughts, the criticisms that had once pressed in on her like a dense fog became more like clouds passing through a blue sky.

Accept them

The opposite of control is acceptance: not acting on every thought or resigning yourself to negativity but responding to your ideas and emotions with an open attitude, paying attention to them and letting yourself experience them. Take 10 deep breaths, and notice what's happening in the moment. This can bring relief, but it won't necessarily make you feel good. In fact, you may realize just how upset you really are. The important thing is to show yourself (and others) some compassion and examine the reality of the situation. What's going on—both internally and externally? When Jeffrey acknowledged and made room for his feelings of frustration and anger rather than rejecting them, quashing them, or taking them out on others, he began to notice their energetic quality. They were a signal that something important was at stake and that he needed to take productive action. Instead of yelling at people, he could make a clear request of a colleague or move swiftly on a pressing issue. The more Jeffrey accepted his anger and brought his curiosity to it, the more it seemed to support rather than undermine his leadership.

Act on your values

When you unhook yourself from your difficult thoughts and emotions, you expand your choices. You can decide to act in a way that aligns with your values. We encourage leaders to focus on the concept of *workability*: Is your response going to serve you and your organization in the long term as well as the short term? Will it help you steer others in a direction that furthers your collective purpose? Are you taking a step toward being the leader you most want to be and living the life you most want to live? The mind's thought stream flows endlessly, and emotions change like the weather, but values can be called on at any time, in any situation.

WHAT ARE YOUR VALUES?

This list is drawn from the Personal Values Card Sort (2001), developed by W. R. Miller, J. C'de Baca, D. B. Matthews, and P. L. Wilbourne, of the University of New Mexico. You can use it to quickly identify the values you hold that might inform a challenging situation at work. When you next make a decision, ask yourself whether it is consistent with these values.

Accuracy	Duty	Justice	Realism
Achievement	Family	Knowledge	Responsibility
Authority	Forgiveness	Leisure	Risk
Autonomy	Friendship	Mastery	Safety
Caring	Fun	Moderation	Self-knowledge
Challenge	Generosity	Nonconformity	Service
Comfort	Genuineness	Openness	Simplicity
Compassion	Growth	Order	Stability
Contribution	Health	Passion	Tolerance
Cooperation	Helpfulness	Popularity	Tradition
Courtesy	Honesty	Power	Wealth
Creativity	Humility	Purpose	
Dependability	Humor	Rationality	

When Cynthia considered her values, she recognized how deeply committed she was to both her family and her work. She loved being with her children, but she also cared passionately about the pursuit of justice. Unhooked from her distracting and discouraging feelings of guilt, she resolved to be guided by her principles. She recognized how important it was to get home for dinner with her family every evening and to resist work interruptions during that time. But she also undertook to make a number of important business trips, some of which coincided with school events that she would have preferred to attend. Confident that her values—not solely her emotions—were guiding her, Cynthia finally found peace and fulfillment.

It's impossible to block out difficult thoughts and emotions. Effective leaders are mindful of their inner experiences but not caught in them. They know how to free up their internal resources and commit to actions that align with their values. Developing emotional agility is no quick fix. Even those who, like Cynthia and Jeffrey, regularly practice the steps we've outlined here will often find themselves hooked. But over time, leaders who become increasingly adept at it are the ones most likely to thrive.

SUSAN DAVID is the CEO of Evidence Based Psychology, a cofounder of the Institute of Coaching, and an instructor in psychology at Harvard University. CHRISTINA CONGLETON is a leadership and change consultant at Axon Leadership and has researched stress and the brain at Massachusetts General Hospital and the University of Denver. She holds a master's in human development and psychology from Harvard University.

Reprinted from *Harvard Business Review*, November 2013 (product #R1311L).

6

Don't Let Power Corrupt You

By Dacher Keltner

n the behavioral research I've conducted over the past 20 years, I've uncovered a disturbing pattern: While people usually gain power through traits and actions that advance the interests of others, such as empathy, collaboration, openness, fairness, and sharing, when they start to feel powerful or enjoy a position of privilege, those qualities begin to fade. The powerful are more likely than other people to engage in rude, selfish, and unethical behavior. The 19th-century historian and politician Lord Acton got it right: Power *does* tend to corrupt.

I call this phenomenon "the power paradox," and I've studied it in numerous settings: colleges, the U.S.

Senate, pro sports teams, and a variety of other professional workplaces. In each I've observed that people rise on the basis of their good qualities, but their behavior grows increasingly worse as they move up the ladder. This shift can happen surprisingly quickly. In one of my experiments, known as "the cookie monster" study, I brought people into a lab in groups of three, randomly assigned one to a position of leadership, and then gave them a group writing task. A half hour into their work, I placed a plate of freshly baked cookies—one for each team member, plus an extra—in front of everyone. In all groups each person took one and, out of politeness, left the extra cookie. The question was: Who would take a second treat, knowing that it would deprive others of the same? It was nearly always the person who'd been named the leader. In addition, the leaders were more likely to eat with their mouths open, lips smacking, and crumbs falling onto their clothes.

Studies show that wealth and credentials can have a similar effect. In another experiment, Paul Piff of UC Irvine and I found that whereas drivers of the least expensive vehicles—Dodge Colts, Plymouth Satellites—*always* ceded the right-of-way to pedestrians in a crosswalk, people driving luxury cars such as BMWs and Mercedes yielded only 54% of the time; nearly half the time they ignored the pedestrian and the law. Surveys of employees in 27 countries have revealed that wealthy individuals are more likely to say it's acceptable to engage in unethical behavior, such as taking bribes or cheating on taxes. And recent research led by Danny Miller at HEC Montréal demonstrated that CEOs with MBAs are more likely than those without MBAs to engage in self-serving behavior that increases their personal compensation but causes their companies' value to decline.

These findings suggest that iconic abuses of power —Jeffrey Skilling's fraudulent accounting at Enron,

Tyco CEO Dennis Kozlowski's illegal bonuses, Silvio Berlusconi's bunga bunga parties, Leona Helmsley's tax evasion—are extreme examples of the kinds of misbehavior to which all leaders, at any level, are susceptible. Studies show that people in positions of corporate power are three times as likely as those at the lower rungs of the ladder to interrupt coworkers, multitask during meetings, raise their voices, and say insulting things at the office. And people who've just moved into senior roles are particularly vulnerable to losing their virtues, my research and other studies indicate.

The consequences can be far-reaching. The abuse of power ultimately tarnishes the reputations of executives, undermining their opportunities for influence. It also creates stress and anxiety among their colleagues, diminishing rigor and creativity in the group and dragging down team members' engagement and performance. In a recent poll of 800 managers and employees in 17 industries, about half the respondents who reported being treated rudely at work said they deliberately decreased their effort or lowered the quality of their work in response.

So how can you avoid succumbing to the power paradox? Through awareness and action.

A need for reflection

A first step is developing greater self-awareness. When you take on a senior role, you need to be attentive to the feelings that accompany your newfound power and to any changes in your behavior. My research has shown that power puts us into something like a manic state, making us feel expansive, energized, omnipotent, hungry for rewards, and immune to risk—which opens us up to rash, rude, and unethical actions. But new studies in neuroscience find that simply by reflecting on those thoughts and emotions—"Hey, I'm feeling as if I should rule the world right now"—we can engage regions of our frontal lobes that help us keep our worst impulses in check. When we recognize and label feelings of joy and confidence, we're less likely to make irrational decisions inspired by them. When we acknowledge feelings of frustration (perhaps because subordinates aren't behaving the way we want), we're less likely to respond in adversarial or confrontational ways.

You can build this kind of self-awareness through everyday mindfulness practices. One approach starts with sitting in a comfortable and quiet place, breathing deeply, and concentrating on the feeling of inhaling and exhaling, physical sensations, or sounds or sights in your environment. Studies show that spending just a few minutes a day on such exercises gives people greater focus and calm, and for that reason techniques for them are now taught in training programs at companies like Google, Facebook, Aetna, General Mills, Ford, and Goldman Sachs.

It's also important to reflect on your demeanor and actions. Are you interrupting people? Do you check your phone when others are talking? Have you told a joke or story that embarrassed or humiliated someone else? Do you swear at the office? Have you ever taken sole credit for a group effort? Do you forget colleagues' names? Are you spending a lot more money than in the past or taking unusual physical risks?

If you answered yes to at least a few of these questions, take it as an early warning sign that you're being tempted into problematic, arrogant displays of power. What may seem innocuous to you probably doesn't to your subordinates. Consider a story I recently heard about a needlessly hierarchical lunch delivery protocol on a cable television writing team. Each day when the team's sandwiches arrived, they were doled out to the writers in order of seniority. In failing to correct this behavior, the group's leaders were almost certainly diminishing its collaborative and creative potential. For a contrast, consider U.S. military mess halls, where the practice is the reverse, as the ethnographer and author Simon Sinek notes in the title of his most recent book, *Leaders Eat Last*. Officers adhere to the policy not to cede authority but to show respect for their troops.

Practicing graciousness

Whether you've already begun to succumb to the power paradox or not, you must work to remember and repeat the virtuous behaviors that helped you rise in the first place. When teaching executives and others in positions of power, I focus on three essential practices—empathy, gratitude, and generosity—that have been shown to sustain benevolent leadership, even in the most cutthroat environments.

For example, Leanne ten Brinke, Chris Liu, Sameer Srivastava, and I found that U.S. senators who used empathetic facial expressions and tones of voice when speaking to the floor got more bills passed than those who used domineering, threatening gestures and tones in their speeches. Research by Anita Woolley of Carnegie Mellon and Thomas Malone of MIT has likewise shown that when teammates subtly signal understanding, engagement, interest, and concern for one another, the team is more effective at tackling hard analytical problems.

Small expressions of gratitude also yield positive results. Studies show that romantic partners who acknowledge each other's value in casual conversation are less likely to break up, that students who receive a pat on the back from their teachers are more likely to take on difficult problems, and that people who express appreciation to others in a newly formed group feel stronger ties to the group months later. Adam Grant of Wharton has found that when managers take the time to thank their employees, those workers are more engaged and productive. And my own research on NBA teams with Michael Kraus of Yale University shows that players who physically display their appreciation—through head raps, bear hugs, and hip and chest bumps—inspire their teammates to play better and win nearly two more games per season (which is both statistically significant and often the difference between making the play-offs and not).

Simple acts of generosity can be equally powerful. Studies show that individuals who share with others in a group—for example, by contributing new ideas or directly assisting on projects not their own—are deemed more worthy of respect and influence and more suitable for leadership. Mike Norton at Harvard Business School has found that when organizations provide an opportunity to donate to charities at work, employees feel more satisfied and productive.

It might seem difficult to constantly follow the ethics of "good power" when you're the boss and responsible for making sure things get done. Not so. Your capacity for empathy, gratitude, and generosity can be cultivated by engaging in simple social behaviors whenever the opportunity presents itself: a team meeting, a client pitch or negotiation, a 360-degree feedback session. Here are a few suggestions.

To practice empathy:

- Ask a great question or two in every interaction, and paraphrase important points that others make.

- Listen with gusto. Orient your body and eyes toward the person speaking, and convey interest and engagement vocally.

- When someone comes to you with a problem, signal concern with phrases such as "I'm sorry" and "That's really tough." Avoid rushing to judgment and advice.

- Before meetings, take a moment to think about the person you'll be with and what is happening in his or her life.

Arturo Bejar, Facebook's director of engineering, is one executive I've seen make empathy a priority as he guides his teams of designers, coders, data specialists, and writers. Watching him at work, I've noticed that his meetings all tend to be structured around a cascade of open-ended questions and that he never fails to listen thoughtfully. He leans toward whoever is speaking and carefully writes down everyone's ideas on a notepad. These small expressions of empathy signal to his team that he understands their concerns and wants them to succeed together.

To practice gratitude:

- Make thoughtful thank-yous a part of how you communicate with others.

- Send colleagues specific and timely emails or notes of appreciation for jobs done well.

- Publicly acknowledge the value that each person contributes to your team, including the support staff.

- Use the right kind of touch—pats on the back, fist bumps, or high fives—to celebrate successes.

When Douglas Conant was CEO of the Campbell Soup Company, he emphasized a culture of gratitude across the organization. Each day he and his executive assistants would spend up to an hour scanning his email and the company intranet for news of employees who were "making a difference." Conant would then personally thank them—everyone from senior executives to maintenance people—for their contributions, usually with handwritten notes. He estimates that he wrote at least 10 a day, for a total of about 30,000 during his decade-long tenure, and says he would often find them pinned up in employees' workspaces. Leaders I've taught have shared other tactics: giving small gifts to employees, taking them out to nice lunches or dinners, hosting employee-of-the-month celebrations, and setting up real or virtual "gratitude walls," on which coworkers can thank one another for specific contributions.

To practice generosity:

- Seek opportunities to spend a little one-on-one time with the people you lead.

- Delegate some important and high-profile responsibilities.

- Give praise generously.

- Share the limelight. Give credit to all who contribute to the success of your team and your organization.

Pixar director Pete Docter is a master of this last practice. When I first started working with him on the movie *Inside Out*, I was curious about a cinematic marvel he'd created five years before: the montage at the start of the film *Up*, which shows the protagonist, Carl, meeting and falling in love with a girl, Ellie; enjoying a long married life with her; and then watching her succumb to illness. When I asked how he'd accomplished it, his answer was an exhaustive list of the 250 writers, animators, actors, story artists, designers, sculptors, editors, programmers, and computer modelers who had worked on it with him. When people ask about the box-office success of *Inside Out*, he gives a similar response. Another Facebook executive I've worked with, product manager Kelly Winters, shares credit in a similar way. When she does PowerPoint presentations or talks to reporters about the success of her Compassion team, she always lists or talks about the data analysts, engineers, and content specialists who made it happen.

You can outsmart the power paradox by practicing the ethics of empathy, gratitude, and generosity. It will bring out the best work and collaborative spirit of those around you. And you, too, will benefit, with a burnished reputation, long-lasting leadership, and the dopamine-rich delights of advancing the interests of others.

DACHER KELTNER is a professor of psychology at the University of California, Berkeley, and the faculty director of the Greater Good Science Center.

Reprinted from *Harvard Business Review*,
October 2016 (product #R1610K).

7

Mindfulness for People Who Are Too Busy to Meditate

By Maria Gonzalez

Mindfulness has become almost a buzzword. But what is it, really? Quite simply, mindfulness is being present and aware, moment by moment, regardless of circumstances.

For instance, researchers have found that practicing mindfulness can reprogram the brain to be more rational and less emotional. When faced with a decision, meditators who practiced mindfulness showed increased activity in the posterior insula of the brain, an area linked to rational decision making. This allowed them to make decisions based more on fact than emotion. This is good news since other research has found that reasoning is actually suffused with emotion—the two are inseparable. What's more, our positive and negative feelings about people, things, and ideas arise much more rapidly than our conscious thoughts—in a matter of milliseconds. We push threatening information away and hold friendly information close. We apply fight-or-flight reflexes not only to predators, but also to data itself.

There are specific techniques that you can practice to help you reap the benefits of mindfulness. You may have heard about a mindfulness-enhancing technique where you meditate for a period of time before going about the rest of your day. This is definitely valuable. But I prefer practicing mindfulness all day, in every circumstance. In essence, you start living all of life mindfully, and over time there is no distinction between your formal mindfulness practice and making a presentation, negotiating a deal, driving your car, working out, or playing a round of golf.

Try a technique I call "micro meditations." These are meditations that can be done several times a day for one to three minutes at a time. Periodically throughout the day, become aware of your breath. It could be when you feel yourself getting stressed or overwhelmed, with too much to do and too little time, or perhaps when you notice yourself becoming increasingly distracted and agitated.

First, notice the quality of your breathing. Is it shallow or deep? Are you holding your breath and in so doing perhaps also holding your stomach? Are you hunching your shoulders?

Next, start breathing so that you are bringing the breath into the belly. Do not strain. If this feels too unnatural, then try bringing the breath down into the lower chest. If the mind wanders, gently come back to the breath—without judging yourself for momentarily losing focus.

You will notice that by regularly practicing this micro meditation you will become more aware and calmer. You'll find yourself to be increasingly mindful, calm, and focused. It's helpful to create reminders for yourself to practice these meditations throughout the day. You can do them two to four times a day, every hour, before you go to a meeting, or whenever you feel like multitasking is eroding your concentration—whatever is feasible and feels right to you. Micro meditations can put you back on track and help you develop your mindfulness muscle.

A second technique I use is one I call "mindfulness in action." Instead of adding a new routine to your day, just experience your day a little differently by paying attention in a particular way, for seconds at a time.

For instance, if you've ever been in a meeting and suddenly noticed that you missed what was just said because you were "somewhere else" for the last few minutes, chances are you weren't being mindful. Maybe you were thinking about your next meeting, everything on your to do list, or an incoming text. Or perhaps you just zoned out. This is incredibly common. Unfortunately, not being present in this way can cause misunderstandings, missed opportunities, and wasted time.

The next time you're in a meeting, try to do nothing but *listen* for seconds at a time. This is harder than it sounds, but with practice you will be able to listen continuously, without a break in concentration. Whenever you notice that your mind has wandered, come right back to listening to the voice of the person who is speaking. You may have to redirect your attention dozens of times in a single meeting—it's extremely common. Always bring yourself back gently and with patience. You are training the mind to be right here, right now.

These techniques can, as I've said, rewire the brain. As a result, three critical things happen. First, your ability to concentrate increases. Second, you see things with increasing clarity, which improves your judgment. And third, you develop equanimity. Equanimity enables you to reduce your physiological and emotional stress and enhances the likelihood that you will be able to find creative solutions to problems.

Practicing mindfulness—and reaping its benefits— doesn't have to be a big time commitment or require special training. You can start right now—in this moment.

MARIA GONZALEZ is the founder and president of Argonauta Consulting. Her most recent book is *Mindful Leadership: The 9 Ways to Self-Awareness, Transforming Yourself, and Inspiring Others*. She has recently launched the Mindful Leadership app.

Adapted from content posted on hbr.org on
March 31, 2014 (product #H00QLQ).

8

Is Something Lost When We Use Mindfulness as a Productivity Tool?

By Charlotte Lieberman

came to mindfulness as a healing practice after overcoming an addiction to the drug Adderall during my junior year of college. I found myself in this situation because I thought that using Adderall to help me focus was no big deal—an attitude shared by 81% of students nationwide.[1]

Adderall simply seemed like an innocuous shortcut to getting things done efficiently and effortlessly. I still remember the rush I felt my first night on Adderall: I completed every page of assigned Faulkner reading (not easy), started and finished a paper several weeks before the due date (because why not?), Swiffered my room (twice), and answered all of my unread emails (even the irrelevant ones). It's also worth noting that I had forgotten to eat all night and somehow found myself still awake at 4 a.m., my jaw clenched and my stomach rumbling. Sleep was nowhere in sight.

What I saw initially as a shortcut to more focus and productivity ultimately turned out instead to be a long detour toward self-destruction. Rather than thinking of focus as the by-product of my own power and capability, I looked outside of myself, thinking that a pill would solve my problems.

Long story short, I eventually came to grips with my problem, got off the drug, and found an antidote to my crippling self-doubt: meditation—particularly, mindfulness (or Vipassana) meditation.

So to me, it's somewhat ironic that mindfulness has taken the media by storm precisely because of its scientifically proven benefits for focus and productivity.[2]

And it's not just because I came to mindfulness as a way of healing from the fallout of the amount of pressure I put on myself to be productive. While mindfulness is not a little blue pill, it's starting to be thought of as a kind of shortcut to focus and productivity, not unlike a morning coffee. A wisdom tradition associated with personal growth and insight is now being absorbed by our culture as a tool for career development and efficiency. But should mindfulness really be used to attain a particular goal? Is it OK to think of a practice that's all about "being" as just another tool for "doing"?

Companies seem to think so. Given the mindfulness buzz, it's no surprise that corporate mindfulness programs are proliferating across the country. Google offers "Search Inside Yourself" classes that teach mindfulness meditation at work. As celebrated in the recent book *Mindful Work* by David Gelles, corporations like Goldman Sachs, HBO, Deutsche Bank, Target, and Bank of America tout the productivity-related benefits of meditation to their employees.

The world of professional athletics—most recently the NFL—too has drawn attention to the achievement-oriented underpinnings of the mainstream mindfulness movement. The 2015 *Wall Street Journal* article that explored the Seattle Seahawks' success in the 2014 Super Bowl explained that the team's secret weapon was its willingness to work with a sports psychologist who teaches mindfulness. Seahawks assistant head coach Tom Cable went so far as to describe the team as "incredibly mindful."

This article was written in January, a month before the Seahawks lost the 2015 Super Bowl. In the wake of their defeat, I heard several conversations among acquaintances and family members (all of whom were sports fans and were nonmeditating but aware of meditation) in which they expressed skepticism about the power of meditation for focus and success. I mean, how much can we embrace mindfulness as a tool for success if a team famous for meditating lost the Super Bowl?

Still a lot, I think. And I'm fine stopping here to admit (if you haven't already concluded yourself) that the commodification of mindfulness as a productivity tool leaves me with a strange taste in my mouth. Above all, I am resistant to the teleological attitude toward meditation: that it's a "tool" designed for a particular purpose, contingent on "results."

And yet asserting this skepticism brings me back to a conversation I had with my vegan cousin a few years ago. He is a PhD student in biological anthropology, an animal activist, and a longtime vegan. When I asked him if he was irked by all the celebrities going vegan to lose weight, he shook his head vigorously. "I'd rather have people do the right thing for the wrong reason than not do the right thing at all," he explained (the "right" thing here being veganism).

This philosophy seems applicable to the mindfulness craze (aka "McMindfulness") too. I'm happy more people are getting the myriad benefits of meditation. I am glad that you're no longer thought of as a patchouli-scented hippie if you're an avid meditator. If corporate mindfulness programs mean that employee self-care is more valued in the workplace, then so be it.

But I also think there's room to consider an alternative way of talking about meditation, especially when it comes to how we relate to our work.

Looking at mindfulness as a tool for accomplishing what we need to get done keeps us trapped in a future-oriented mindset, rather than encouraging us to dilate the present moment. Of course, this doesn't invalidate the neuroscience; mindfulness helps us get more stuff done. But what about allowing mindfulness to just be? To have the effects it is going to have, without attaching a marketing pitch to this ancient practice?

Psychologist Kristin Neff is renowned for coining the term "self-compassion." In particular, Neff has asserted that the first component of self-compassion is kindness, the ability to shrug off those times when we "let ourselves down," when we don't get to check off everything from our to do lists. The other two components of self-compassion are awareness and mindfulness. The goal is not to get more done but to understand that we are enough—and that our worth is not contingent on what we get done. (Although studies have shown that self-forgiveness actually helps us procrastinate less.[3])

I'm not an idealist. I'm not saying everyone should start "Om-ing," devoting themselves solely to self-compassion, and forgetting all about their to do lists. But I am saying that compassion, and self-compassion, ought to move into the foreground as we talk about mindfulness—even in corporate mindfulness programs.

There's no shame in wanting to be productive at work. But there's also no shame in being able to cut yourself some slack, to extend yourself some love during those times at work when things don't feel so great.

CHARLOTTE LIEBERMAN is a New York–based writer and editor.

Notes

1. A. D. DeSantis and A. C. Hane, "'Adderall Is Definitely Not a Drug': Justifications for the Illegal Use of ADHD Stimulants," *Substance Use and Misuse* 45, no. 1–2 (2010): 31–46.
2. D. M. Levy et al., "The Effects of Mindfulness Meditation Training on Multitasking in a High-Stress Information Environment," Graphics Interface Conference, 2012.
3. M. J. A. Wohl et al., "I Forgive Myself, Now I Can Study: How Self-Forgiveness for Procrastinating Can Reduce Future Procrastination," *Personality and Individual Differences* 48 (2010): 803–808.

Adapted from content posted on hbr.org on
August 25, 2015 (product #H02AJ1).

9

There Are Risks to Mindfulness at Work

By David Brendel

Mindfulness is close to taking on cult status in the business world. But as with any rapidly growing movement—regardless of its potential benefits—there is good reason here for caution.

Championed for many years by pioneering researchers such as Ellen Langer and Jon Kabat-Zinn, mindfulness is a mental orientation and set of strategies for focusing one's mind on here-and-now experiences, such as abdominal muscle movements during respiration or the chirping of birds outside one's window. It is rooted in ancient Eastern philosophies, such as Taoism and Buddhism. Contemporary empirical research demonstrates its benefits for reducing anxiety and mental stress.[1] A recent study suggested that it might cut the risk of stroke and heart attack as well.

Mindful meditation and related practices are now widely accepted. For example, the *New Republic* published an article entitled "How 2014 Became the Year of Mindfulness." Mindfulness has also recently been featured on CBS's *60 Minutes* and been lauded by the *Huffington Post*. Dan Harris, a well-known ABC News correspondent, has published a best-selling book called *Ten Percent Happier*, which describes his journey to discovering mindful meditation as an optimal way to manage his very publicly shared anxiety disorder. There is increasing interest in how mindfulness can be applied in clinical medicine and psychology, and some large insurance companies are even beginning to consider providing coverage for mindfulness strategies for certain patients.

As an executive coach and physician, I often sing the praises of mindfulness practices and recommend them to clients to manage stress, avoid burnout, enhance leadership capacity, and steady the mind when in the midst of making important business decisions, career transitions, and personal life changes. Drawing on concepts from Eastern philosophies and research evidence from contemporary neuroscience, I help some clients employ controlled breathing and similar strategies in our sessions and in their everyday lives.[2] I also refer clients to trusted colleagues who teach yoga and mindful meditation in greater depth than I can provide in my coaching sessions.

But my growing knowledge of (and enthusiasm for) mindfulness is now tempered by a concern about its potential excesses and the risk that it may be crowding out other equally important models and strategies for managing stress, achieving peak performance, and reaching professional and personal fulfillment. At times, it appears that we are witnessing the development of a "cult of mindfulness" that, if not appropriately recognized and moderated, may result in an unfortunate backlash against it. Here are a couple of my concerns.

The avoidance risk

Some people use mindfulness strategies to avoid critical thinking tasks. I've worked with clients who, instead of rationally thinking through a career challenge or ethical dilemma, prefer to disconnect from their challenges and retreat into a meditative mindset. The issue here is that some problems require more thinking, not less. Sometimes stress is a signal that we need to consider our circumstances through greater self-reflective thought, not a "mindful" retreat to focused breathing or other immediate sensory experiences. Mindfulness strategies can prime the mind for sounder rational thinking—but the former clearly should not displace the latter. One of my clients spent so much time meditating and "mindfully" accepting her life "on its own terms" that she failed to confront underperforming workers (and discipline or fire the worst offenders) in her company. After periods of meditating, she struggled to return to focused, task-oriented thinking. She required significant reminders and reassurance from me that embracing Buddhist meditation does not entail tolerating substandard performance from her employees. Mindful meditation should always be used in the service of enhancing, not displacing, people's rational and analytical thought processes about their careers and personal lives.

The groupthink risk

As mindfulness practices enter mainstream American life, some organizations and companies are admirably encouraging their people to make use of them in the workplace.[3] But I'm aware of situations where this new orientation has gone too far. In one case, the director of a business unit in a financial services corporation required his direct reports to participate several times per week in a 10- to 15-minute mindfulness session that involved controlled breathing and guided imagery. Many participants came to dread the exercise. Some of them felt extremely awkward and uncomfortable, believing that mindfulness practices should be done in private. The very exercise that was supposed to reduce their work-related stress actually had increased it. The practice continued for weeks until several members of the group finally gathered the courage to tell the group leader that they would strongly prefer the daily exercises be optional, with impunity for nonparticipants. Mindfulness is rooted in a philosophy and psychology of self-efficacy and proactive self-care. Imposing it on people in a top-down manner degrades the practice and the people who might benefit from using it of their own volition.

That mindfulness has emerged as a major cultural phenomenon on the contemporary American scene and in the business world in particular can be good news for people dealing with stress, burnout, and other realities of the modern workplace. But mindfulness practices need to be incorporated as one among many self-chosen strategies for people aiming to cope with stress, think effectively, make sound decisions, and achieve fulfillment. Mindfulness practices should be used to enhance our rational and ethical thinking processes, not limit or displace them. And mindfulness practices should never be imposed on people, especially in the workplace. At its very core, mindfulness will be a huge step forward for Western culture if it stays focused on creating opportunities for individuals to discover their own personalized strategies for taming anxieties, managing stress, optimizing work performance, and reaching happiness and fulfillment.

DAVID BRENDEL is an executive coach, leadership development specialist, and psychiatrist based in Boston. He is founder and director of Leading Minds Executive Coaching and a cofounder of Strategy of Mind, a leadership development and coaching company.

Notes

1. J. Corliss, "Mindfulness Meditation May Ease Anxiety, Mental Stress," *Harvard Health Blog*, January 8, 2014.
2. M. Baime, "This Is Your Brain on Mindfulness," *Shambhala Sun*, July 2011, 44–84; and "Relaxation Techniques: Breath Control Helps Quell Errant Stress Response," *Harvard Health Publications*, January 2015.
3. A. Huffington, "Mindfulness, Meditation, Wellness and Their Connection to Corporate America's Bottom Line," *Huffington Post*, March 18, 2013.

Adapted from content posted on hbr.org on
February 11, 2015 (product #H01VIF).

Index